CW00508845

Lovers

A play

Tony Rushforth

Samuel French — London
www.samuelfrench-london.co.uk

© 2012 by Tony Rushforth

Rights of Performance by Amateurs are controlled by Samuel French Ltd, 52 Fitzroy Street, London W1T 5JR, and they, or their authorized agents, issue licences to amateurs on payment of a fee. **It is an infringement of the Copyright to give any performance or public reading of the play before the fee has been paid and the licence issued.**

The Royalty Fee indicated below is subject to contract and subject to variation at the sole discretion of Samuel French Ltd.

Basic fee for each and every
performance by amateurs   Code D
in the British Isles

The publication of this play does not imply that it is necessarily available for performance by amateurs or professionals, either in the British Isles or Overseas. Amateurs and professionals considering a production are strongly advised in their own interests to apply to the appropriate agents for written consent before starting rehearsals or booking a theatre or hall.

ISBN 978 0 573 12149 4

The right of Tony Rushforth to be identified as author of this work has been asserted by him in accordance with Section 77 of the Copyright, Designs and Patents Act 1988. Please see page iv for further copyright information

LOVERS

First performed at the Questors Theatre, Ealing, on November 4th 2011 with the following cast:

Maureen	Wendy Megeney
Bob	Robin Ingram
Anna	Helen Walker

Directed by Tony Rushforth
Set Design by Bron Blake

CHARACTERS

Maureen, 46
Bob, mid 60s
Anna, mid / late 30s

The action of the play takes place in a section of a graveyard in the small town of Threshton in the North Yorkshire Dales

Time — the present

COPYRIGHT INFORMATION
(See also page ii)

This play is fully protected under the Copyright Laws of the British Commonwealth of Nations, the United States of America and all countries of the Berne and Universal Copyright Conventions.

All rights, including Stage, Motion Picture, Radio, Television, Public Reading, and Translation into Foreign Languages, are strictly reserved.

No part of this publication may lawfully be reproduced in ANY form or by any means — photocopying, typescript, recording (including video-recording), manuscript, electronic, mechanical, or otherwise — or be transmitted or stored in a retrieval system, without prior permission.

Licences are issued subject to the understanding that it shall be made clear in all advertising matter that the audience will witness an amateur performance; that the names of the authors of the plays shall be included on all announcements and on all programmes; and that the integrity of the authors' work will be preserved.

The Royalty Fee is subject to contract and subject to variation at the sole discretion of Samuel French Ltd.

In Theatres or Halls seating Four Hundred or more the fee will be subject to negotiation.

In Territories Overseas the fee quoted in this Acting Edition may not apply. A fee will be quoted on application to our local authorized agent, or if there is no such agent, on application to Samuel French Ltd, London.

VIDEO-RECORDING OF AMATEUR PRODUCTIONS

Please note that the copyright laws governing video-recording are extremely complex and that it should not be assumed that any play may be video-recorded for *whatever purpose* without first obtaining the permission of the appropriate agents. The fact that a play is published by Samuel French Ltd does not indicate that video rights are available or that Samuel French Ltd controls such rights.

PRODUCTION NOTES

Maureen, Bob and Anna speak to Michael as if he were actually present.

The stage directions are only stated as a guide, which the director, designer and actors can freely interpret.

For Maureen and Bob the text is not written in a precise regional dialect. Maureen has an educated Dublin accent, but has not lived there for some 22 years, and although Bob comes from North Yorkshire, care must be taken not to overstate his accent which might push the character into Yorkshire "stereotype".

Other plays by Tony Rushforth
published by Samuel French Ltd:

Voyager
The Kerry Dance
Seascape

For Joseph and Orla

LOVERS

A section of a graveyard in the small town of Threshton, North Yorkshire Dales. Early summer

The focus is Michael's grave which is slightly raised and set at an angle. The audience sees it from the back of the low headstone and the stone surround which encloses grey chippings and includes a fixed, metal vase containing dried flowers, three dried-up wreaths and windswept leaves and twigs. There are two principal entrances and exits to the graveyard which are referred to as the upper and the lower path. Whether we see a couple more headstones is up to the staging and the designer, however we might see a section of an old Yorkshire stone wall against which some small branches give evidence of the previous night's storm. Nearby is an open meshed litter bin which contains some rotting flowers and a couple of wreaths and DR is a new roll of plastic wire netting. A little further away is a wooden bench upon which we can see Maureen's shopping basket, handbag and an enamel jug of water. There are a pair of gloves behind the bench and two small bunches of white roses on the bench next to the basket

Some expanse of grey sky would help to create this bleak location. Throughout the play during Maureen, Anna and Bob's "private" exchanges with Michael the general lighting level is reduced and light is slightly intensified on the grave

When the play opens we hear distant thunder followed by a tolling bell which fades as the Lights come up centred on Bob and Maureen saying the rosary. Maureen is UC of Michael's grave and is 46 years old but looks older; she doesn't wear make-up. She is wearing a warm coat and scarf and is dressed in a nondescript but tidy fashion. Bob is in his mid 60s. He is kneeling slightly upstage of Maureen and is wearing his working overalls and an old open jacket and muffler and dirty Wellington boots. UC *is Bob's wheelbarrow which contains tools and some wooden stakes for fencing repairs*

Bob Holy Mary, mother of God, pray for us sinners, now and at the hour of our death.

Bob } (*together*) Amen.
Maureen

Maureen Hail Mary, full of grace, the Lord is with thee. Blessed art thou among women and blessed is the fruit of thy womb, Jesus.

Bob Holy Mary, mother of God, pray for us sinners, now and at the hour of our death.

Bob } (*together*) Amen.
Maureen

Maureen (*kissing the cross on her rosary beads and making the sign of the cross*) In the name of the Father and of the Son, and of the Holy Spirit.

Bob } (*together*) Amen.
Maureen

The general lighting fades in as Maureen puts her rosary beads in her coat pocket and smiles at Bob. She picks up two wreaths which Bob takes from her. In this sequence Bob has to ensure that the scene is well paced. Throughout he does his best to reassure Maureen, to comfort her, to give her confidence and to remind her of happier days

Bob Sorry, Maureen. I didn't like moving them.

Maureen looks at him

   Not until you came up. But after last night I was going to tidy up the surround ... such a mess.

Bob takes the wreaths to the litter bin

Maureen I didn't expect you to.
Bob You've caught me out ... didn't think you'd come up today of all days.
Maureen (*politely*) Still got Joe to do the digging?
Bob Couldn't manage without him. In any case, at my age, I need help — and there's the presbytery garden. And now after the storm ... side gate needs repairing — oh, you should just see it up at top, fences are down, they'll have to be repaired — sheep'll get in.

Bob puts the wreaths in the litter bin

Maureen They said it was gale force in Harrogate ... on the news.
Bob Aye ... I'm not surprised, all in all we were lucky.
Maureen (*after a pause*) It woke me up ... I heard some thunder ... didn't ... didn't like it ...
Bob I know, it's all right, Maureen, it's all over. Weather forecast says today we're going to see some sun. Can you believe it?
Maureen (*totally preoccupied*) I was having a ... a dream ... I'd put on my coat ... left the house ... and I'd come up here ... I was that upset ... And then, then I woke up. (*Beat*) I was kneeling at the foot of the bed looking down at the grave ... and that's when I must have heard the thunder ... it woke me up.
Bob You mustn't upset yourself ...
Maureen You know what it's like, for a minute or two you just don't know where you are ... then ... then I saw the dressing table and the mirror ... (*she sighs*) so I knew. I got back into bed, pulled the bedclothes round me and tried to sleep ... but I couldn't. It all kept going through my mind ... the dream ... what did it mean? Then of course I realized ... that's why I'm here. After *all this time* I've come up to see Michael ... to see the gravestone.
Bob Well ... I'm glad you're here.

Maureen It was because I didn't want to see the earth, the coffin
in the earth ... like it was at the funeral. (*She crosses to the
bench and gets her small brush and dustpan and a newspaper
from her basket*)

Bob They can't do it straight away, it takes time ...

Maureen looks at him

The gravestone ... the surround ... the earth has to settle.

Maureen Just couldn't face it. Don't know how many times
I've tried ... once I got as far as the church ... and then ... then
went back home. Not being able to face me own husband's
grave ... Pathetic.

Bob No it's not. (*Beat*) Father Keegan was concerned ... he
asked ...

Maureen looks at him

Asked if you'd been up.

Maureen Did he? (*She crosses back to the grave with dustpan
and brush and newspaper*) Well at least he let Michael be
buried here.

Bob looks at her

He wasn't practising, you know, you must have noticed.
(*Strongly*) But he believed, yes, I know he did.

Bob Faith's a private matter, Maureen, between you and your
conscience.

Maureen (*pointedly*) It depends on the conscience.

*Maureen puts down the newspaper, kneels and picks up two
dried-up bunches of flowers. Bob takes them from her and takes
them to the litter bin. Maureen starts to brush the leaves and
twigs from the surround*

Bob Leave it, I'll give you a hand later.

Maureen Thanks, Bob, but I want to do it myself.

Bob Right. (*He puts the flowers in the litter bin and comes back to the grave*) It doesn't seem long since he joined the team. Scrum half, weekly training and straight into the top league. We had some good times ... and he knew when to stop.

Maureen It was my fault.

Bob looks at her

That he gave it up. All those away matches. I didn't like being on my own ... not even then.

Bob None of us like being on our own, Maureen. (*He smiles*) I learned years ago that Red Lion wasn't the answer.

Maureen Except on Saturday?

Bob looks at her

I didn't mind him seeing you.

Bob We just had a chat — the one pint. Disagreed about politics, caught up on the ... the "sporting news".

Maureen (*crossing to her basket for a plastic bag*) You shouldn't be on your own, Bob. I thought you and Clare Robins would have made a go of it.

Bob That was a long time ago.

Maureen Faint heart ...?

Bob No. It just didn't happen ... and then suddenly ... you can't believe it ... suddenly you're thinking about retirement.

Maureen (*returning to the grave*) Too set in your ways.

Bob Aye. You couldn't say that about Michael.

Maureen (*meaningfully*) No, you couldn't. (*She kneels and brushes the leaves and twigs into the plastic bag*)

Bob What do they say nowadays? He was his own man.

Maureen Every Friday ... waiting for the car to come round the corner, supper in the oven, sometimes dried up because he was so late.

Bob Friday night traffic, Maureen.

Maureen I know. I didn't want him taking any risks.

Bob (*surveying the grave*) He was no age, no age at all. You've done him proud, it's very er ... tasteful. No big headstone, just the surround.

Maureen (*rising and taking the plastic bag to the litter bin*) Nowadays you get a lot of that black marble and gold lettering.

Bob Aye. Bit flashy. (*Beat*) He was very much respected, Maureen ... that must have been a comfort. It was a big funeral.

Maureen I hadn't expected so many.

Bob Three came up from the London office.

Maureen Yes, I spoke to some of them ...

Bob A lot of local people, Conservative Club, Threshton Rugby Club, Ilkley Rotary. (*He suddenly sees something in the distance and takes a pace* DR) And that tree's come down — Bishop planted it last year. Just doesn't make sense ... end of June. Global warming, well that's what they say.

Maureen takes a pace forward and looks down to the lower part of the graveyard — they are standing side by side

Maureen Just now, on my way up ... saw the graves ... saw names of people going way back.

Bob Aye, it's a constant reminder. (*Beat*) But it makes you think you know working here. I never thought death would be my living, if you see what I mean.

Maureen They sold the Hall — what could you do? Father Keegan was glad to take you on, he's been very fortunate.

Bob (*looking round*) He calls this the new plot ... but there's not a lot of room. Now up at top there's nearly an acre.

Maureen (*not listening*) When I came up ... it's as if I hadn't noticed they'd gone ... people I knew ...

Bob (*pointing out front*) Old Eva Dobson ... funeral last month ...

Maureen In charge of the kitchen.

Bob (*chuckling*) Very much in charge. Very particular about my vegetables.

Maureen (*smiling*) She liked your asparagus.

Bob (*enjoying the compliment*) You mean Lady Talbot did. (*Beat*) You were the youngest housekeeper we'd ever had ... all the way from Dublin. When they stopped saying Mass at the Hall you came down here, chauffeur driven. I remember the first time ... all the fellers noticed you but Michael beat 'em to it. (*Smiling*) Rest of 'em had no chance, no chance at all.

Maureen (*reproving*) Don't be ridiculous. (*She crosses back to the grave*) I was young ... that's all it was, I was young. (*Resentfully*) And look at me now, I've grown old before my time.

Bob Don't you be ridiculous. (*Beat*) Do you remember he asked you out ... to the St Patrick's Night ... with the ceilidh band ...? (*He laughs*) Swept you off your feet. Michael was like that. He certainly knew how to turn on the charm ...

Maureen Charisma, they call it now. (*She picks up the dustpan and brush*)

Bob Yes, he had plenty of that. And he didn't waste any time, Maureen. It was a "whirlwind" courtship ... what was it the priest used to say ...?

Maureen "When friendship has ripened into courtship." (*She crosses to the bench*)

Bob Haven't heard that in years.

Maureen Nowadays there isn't really a courtship, they just go and live with each other ...

Bob And find out if they want to spend the rest of their lives together.

During the following Maureen puts the dustpan and brush in her basket and sits and takes out a small bottle of water and drinks

Maureen At least they have a rehearsal for the real thing. Maybe that's a good idea, find out if you want to spend a lifetime together, if you are ... compatible. Big decision. "The real thing" — what is it? We used to call it love.

Bob (*smiling*) They still do. (*Beat*) Are you all right?

Maureen I'm fine ...

Bob When you've been to Thomas's grave, call in at the shed — make some tea.

Maureen I'll see how I feel.

Bob Michael should have given up the London job ... it was too much of a strain ... driving up every weekend and you ... not well. But he wanted you to be secure, it was a good salary.

Maureen Money isn't everything.

Bob I know, but he thought the world of you.

Maureen (*looking at him*) Did he?

Bob You know he did.

Pause

Maureen I haven't been able to cry.

Bob You need more time.

Maureen I didn't need time to cry for Thomas ... we'd waited such a long time for him. You know I still thought we would have another, Father Keegan said I mustn't despair, it was a cross I would have to bear. (*Beat*) I used to sneak up to church without Michael knowing and call out and ask ... (*distressed*) ... why me? ... Why me? What did I expect? A miracle?

Bob (*crossing to the bench*) You mustn't upset yourself ... it was a long time ago.

Maureen I kept all Thomas's things in the spare room ready ... waiting ... I'd redecorated it, moved the cot, felt I had to ... put it in the corner. I folded the baby clothes neatly in the chest of drawers, put fresh lavender from the garden between the clothes ... but the miracle didn't happen.

Bob You weren't well.

Maureen They gave me those pills ... it was as if ... as if I was cut off ... in a world of my own.

Bob Now then. You're much better now. I'm right glad. And those evening classes are helping.

Maureen picks up one of the small bunches of white roses

Maureen (*suddenly reassured*) Yes they are. Yes ... I'm much better. (*Beat*) I've brought Michael these roses ... they got battered last night.

Bob They look grand ... well ... I must take this stuff up for 't fence. Joe said he'd be here tomorrow by seven-thirty — (*he chuckles*) — but you know what Joe's like. And when you've been to Thomas's grave — think on, make yourself a cuppa.

Maureen I might.

Bob Right.

Bob looks at her, concerned, and exits to the upper path with the wheelbarrow

Maureen picks up the jug of water, kneels at the grave and pours the water in the vase

Maureen (*talking to the headstone*) I don't want people thinking I'm neglecting you. I'm sure they had plenty to say when I was in the hospital. But that's ... all over, thank God. Now I'm all right. I've had to be ... *you* know that, Michael ... I've had to be strong, very strong. I've kept saying to myself — mustn't go under again — in spite of everything — *I mustn't*. (*She arranges the roses*) This was the first thing I planted after we moved ... when it was the new house. I was so thrilled ... you called it the Maureen Rose, *my* Maureen Rose you said ... and you held me in your arms and I laughed and cried ... I was so happy. (*Pause*) I've put a brave face on it, I had to, *on all of it*, Michael. And then the phone call from the office, it was so sudden ... there was no time to talk, so many things left unsaid ... and now it's too late. (*Pause*) I know I wasn't ... wasn't a passionate woman. I'm sorry if I let you down ... but I did love you, you know that. (*Beat*) I keep thinking about what you said when I told you I was pregnant with Thomas. You said he was our love child. Did you really mean that, Michael? *Did you?* It was such a lovely thing to say ... if you meant it. (*She rises*) Anyway ... I've brought some roses for Thomas. ... He would have been five today. (*She crosses to the bench with the empty jug, picks up the shopping basket, handbag and the other bunch of roses*) I'll go down ... see if he's all right.

Maureen exits to the lower path

There is the sound of rooks in the trees and then the church clock strikes four o' clock

Anna, who comes from London, enters from the upper path, crosses a couple of paces towards Maureen's exit, then goes to Michael's grave. She is attractive and in her mid/late thirties, has a natural intelligence and can sometimes be feisty. She wears make-up and fashionable clothes which show off her figure. She carries a leather handbag over her shoulder

Anna (*controlling her emotions*) So this is it. All on your own. This is where you are.

Pause

God, it's cold here, Mike. (*She looks in the direction of the lower path*) I waited until she went ... Maureen. She didn't see me. She looked older than the photo. I felt so stupid hiding behind that bloody angel ... up there, painted on the marble — in gold. Must have cost a fortune. (*Beat*) Mike ... when I didn't hear from you ... I thought something had happened *to her,* not you. It was one hell of a shock, I just couldn't take it in. (*Beat*) No ... no ... I'm not going to cry.

Bob enters from the top path to collect the roll of plastic wire netting but stops short when he hears Anna speak and virtually drops the wire netting

Anna Hello, Bob.
Bob *Anna!* Anna. I wrote to you, asked you ...

Bob's tone in this scene must show that he strongly resents Anna

Anna Been a long time, Bob. Last year's match ... Twickenham?
Bob I asked you not to come, for Maureen's sake.

Anna (*looking at the grave*) I just had to see ... for myself. (*To Bob*) You haven't changed ... you were never on my side, were you?

Bob I tried to make Mike see sense ... he was married to a good woman who was ill ... very ill.

Anna I wasn't unsympathetic if that's what you mean. All things considered I've been ... I've been very tolerant. (*Beat*) Mike always said that he wouldn't leave her until she was discharged ... capable of looking after herself, that's what he promised.

Bob (*cynically*) "Care in the community"? You're out of touch.

Anna Well it's not like living in a city ... he said they had good neighbours.

Bob Neighbours don't want the responsibility ——

Anna (*overlapping*) Bob, once she was out of hospital I didn't put any pressure on him ... for six months. But I'm no bloody saint. I said I'd waited long enough and that he'd got to make a decision and stop farting around. Just before he drove off that last time, I told him. I said I can't take any more. He knew I meant it.

Bob I know. He told me ... said he was being pulled in every direction. I could see it in his face ... like a wounded animal ...

Anna For heaven's sake ... (*She takes out cigarettes and lighter from her handbag and lights one*)

Bob Can't you get it into your head that he didn't want to hurt Maureen *any more*. After Thomas died he felt guilty for deciding to work in London. I told him not to but he couldn't resist promotion. Maureen struggled on for nearly two years and then tried to end it all, it was as serious as that. But he'd met you ... and then you had the trump card ... you had Jamie.

Anna I'm not going to take responsibility for Maureen's breakdown. Look at it from my point of view, every Friday he was off on the M1, the long drive "home". But his home was with me and Jamie. No. It was make your mind up time. I said if not for me then he should do it for Jamie.

Bob I've told you — he didn't want to hurt Maureen. (*Beat*) Anyroad I'm glad you didn't bring the lad.

Anna I didn't want him to see the grave ... he's too young. I want him to remember Mike as his dad, playing games, telling stories, going to the park. (*Beat*) Bob, I wouldn't have taken Jamie away from him, I wouldn't. God, he loved that boy ... sometimes he would get away from the office early so that he could take him out, on his own — I think he was trying to make up for being away at weekends.

Bob He thought you might leave him.

Anna No, I wouldn't have left him, I just wanted to bring him to his senses, make him come to a decision.

Bob Emotional blackmail?

Anna I was desperate ... he was living two lives. It had to stop ... and the last time I saw him I told him Maureen had to be told.

Pause

Bob He didn't tell her.

Anna You're sure?

Bob She wouldn't have been able to keep it to herself ... she would have told me.

Anna looks at him

I've known her for a very long time, she would have. (*Beat*) I was grateful, Anna, that you didn't come to the funeral.

Anna Don't be. It would have been too painful, humiliating. Can you imagine me standing at the back of the church like a fucking acquaintance.

Bob (*quietly*) Anna ... that's enough. But you mustn't meet her, she's just gone down to Thomas's grave.

Anna Don't worry, I won't stay. What's the point ...? I shouldn't have come. (*Looking at the grave*) Mike's gone ... I won't ever see him again.

Bob You have your faith.

Anna I lost it a long time ago. But you're right ... why meet her? The satisfaction of telling? ... What purpose would it serve? No, I'm better than that. (*She meets Bob's eye*) What the eye doesn't see? (*She stubs out the cigarette. To herself*) I really should stop.

Bob crosses to get the plastic wire

Bob Have you come by car?

Anna Couldn't face it. Train to Leeds and then the bus.

Bob (*looking at his watch*) You've got a long wait, next bus is an hour but Castle Café's open and it's next to the bus stop.

Anna Right. That'll warm me up.

Bob Anna? So that you don't meet her, (*he gestures in the direction of the upper path*) go through back gate and down to cattle market.

Anna That's the way I came. So this is how it ends ... I can't believe it. (*Beat*) You meant a lot to him ... he often talked about you.

Bob Did he?

Anna Often ... rugby ... the old times.

Bob I tried to look after him.

Anna You did.

Pause

Bob (*firmly*) Goodbye, Anna.

Anna Give me a minute ... I want to be on my own ...

Bob All right ... *don't be long*.

Bob exits to the upper path taking the roll of plastic wire

Anna moves to the grave

Anna Jamie keeps asking about you ... I can't bring myself to say that you're dead, he's too young to understand. (*She crosses to the bench and opens her bag and during the follow-*

ing takes out the drawing and leaves the bag on the corner of the bench) Mother said I should tell him that you're in heaven with the angels ... can you imagine me saying that? Anyway ... I can't keep putting it off. I've brought you his drawing ... the one that he did at the nursery ... you know the one that he said was Mummy and Daddy ... and you teased me because he drew you twice my size. (*She folds the picture and puts it under the "marble" chippings*) But it comforts me to do it ... (*near to tears*) ... it bloody well comforts me. (*Pause*) I keep seeing you on that night when we met in the pub, I couldn't take my eyes off you, and you knew it ... just before you left you smiled back at me, and that did it. You didn't waste much time, you came in the next night — thank God it was my shift, and you asked me out for supper ... then the following week ... you came back to the flat ... (*Pause, then with anger*) Why am I talking like this? (*She rises*) I don't believe you're here ... I don't believe you're anywhere ... you've just, just gone ... that's why I didn't send any flowers — there seemed no point — listen to me, I'm doing it again ... (*She brushes some dust from the marble chippings from her skirt*)

Maureen enters from the lower path carrying her handbag

Warm light intensifies on the area of the bench

Maureen (*as she crosses to the bench*) Hello.
Anna (*nodding, beat then embarrassed*) Hello.
Maureen (*picking up her gloves behind the bench*) I'm always doing this ... leaving my gloves.

Anna smiles

And the sun's come out, isn't that lovely? (*She crosses to the far side of the grave which now separates them, stops and turns*) Do I know you?
Anna We've not met.
Maureen You knew Michael?

Anna Yes.

Maureen Did you work with him?

Anna Er ... yes.

Maureen The London office?

Anna Yes.

Maureen I am his wife.

Anna I'm sorry.

Maureen. He used to talk to me about people in the office. And your name?

Anna Anna.

Pause

Maureen *Anna*?

Anna Anna Russell.

Maureen Anna.

Anna Yes ... did he mention me?

Maureen No, he didn't. I met some of the others ... at the funeral: Joe Banks, Ian Storey and of course the dreaded Mr Stafford ... (*looking at Anna*) ... so many stories.

Anna Yes.

Maureen Strange, isn't it, that he didn't mention you.

Pause

   That he didn't mention "Anna."

Anna I hadn't worked there very long.

Maureen In the office.

Anna Three months.

Maureen Three months.

Anna Yes.

Maureen You're very attractive.

Anna Thank you.

Maureen I thought you would be.

Anna I don't understand.

Maureen I think you do.

Anna (*pacing towards the bench*) I've told you, I worked with
    ... Michael.

Maureen *No*. You *lived* with Michael ... from Monday to Friday.

Anna is dumbfounded and sits on the bench

Taken your breath away? (*Pause*) I found an email that hadn't
    been deleted.

Anna When?

Maureen Six months ago. (*Beat*) I went on a computer course —
    part of my "therapy". (*She crosses to just behind the bench*) At
    first I didn't tell Michael, wanted to keep it a surprise. I would
    go into Ilkley, the internet café, keep in touch with my cousin
    — she's in Australia. (*She puts her handbag on the bench*)
    Then one weekend he brought up his laptop, he didn't often do
    that. So when he went to the pub I used it, thought I was very
    clever, I brought up the emails and there was this message ...
    in the "Inbox"... staring me in the face, *your* message, I know
    it by heart: "Missing you already. Reached out last night ...
    the bed was cold. Love you, Anna." I read it ... I don't know
    how many times. I wish I hadn't because there was no turning
    back. I couldn't get it out of my head.

Anna You didn't say anything to Mike?

Maureen looks at her

Sorry — he was always Mike to me, I never called him
    Michael.

Maureen I always did — it's a lovely name. (*Beat*) No, I didn't
    say anything. When I thought about it ... it all added up ... it
    seemed to make sense.

Anna Make sense?

Maureen Michael not wanting to move to London. I kept asking
    him to. It didn't have anything to do with house prices, that
    was a convenient excuse. I don't know why I didn't suspect.
    And then there was another message that made it clear that he
    was living with you.

Anna (*critically*) You — went on — reading — the email?

Maureen No. Once I'd told him about the course he kept the laptop in the car. Frightened I suppose.

Anna (*challenging*) Why didn't you tell him that you knew ... about me?

Maureen At first I thought if I keep quiet and don't make an issue of it then it'll fade away, he'll get tired of the "arrangement". After all, it must have been a big strain, the lies, keeping up appearances, running two homes ... for how long?

Anna Just over a year.

Pause

Maureen I hadn't realized it was as long as that. (*Beat*) And so I thought ... yes ... yes, I can cope with this, I can wait, however long it takes ... he'll eventually tire of this other woman, this "Anna".

Anna It was different for me. I knew about you ...

Maureen *You knew*?

Anna From the very beginning.

Maureen I hadn't counted on that. If he could deceive me then I thought he could deceive you. It's so easy to lie.

Anna Until you get found out. When you found out about me you could have tried to make contact. Have it out with me.

Maureen. How could I? Apart from the office I only had his mobile number ... said he didn't want the expense of a phone in the bedsit.

Anna That was one of the rules ... not to answer his mobile.

Maureen Believe me once I'd read that email there were so many times when I wanted to blow his cover, surprise you and shame him.

Anna He wanted to tell you but he just couldn't.

Maureen Frightened I might try again ... end it all?

Anna *Yes*.

Maureen (*distressed*) He was right. Mortal sin or not — without his visits I would have gone under. You should have seen the patients, the state of the wards. Michael kept me sane. I loved him, you see.

Anna (*after a beat*) We both did.

Maureen looks at her. Anna takes out her cigarettes and offers them to Maureen who shakes her head

Do you mind?
Maureen No.
Anna I shouldn't. Started when I was a student, a "mature" student ... now I'm hooked. (*She lights her cigarette*)

Maureen watches her

Maureen In my mind I've often rehearsed this meeting, wondering how I would behave, what I'd say ... but the reality's very different. (*Beat*) Make no mistake about it I have hated you for a long time.
Anna I'm sorry.

The tension between them strongly mounts

Maureen It's easy for you to say that now that Michael's dead, now that you can't claim him, can't take him over completely.
Anna I had come to the end of my tether ...
Maureen End of *your* tether?
Anna Do you think it was easy for me? Knowing from the start that I had to share him ... disappearing every weekend, living his "other" life.
Maureen That was your choice.
Anna No. Mike's choice. You can't take him out of the equation ... that's just too easy, too comforting. You're in denial.
Maureen *In denial!* I was his wife.
Anna And what was I? (*Cynically*) "The other woman"?
Maureen As far as I was concerned you were. But remember, he stayed by me. Every weekend he came to the hospital.
Anna Yes, I know. Perhaps his visits helped to salve his conscience?

Maureen How dare you belittle —— (*She picks up her bag and crosses a few paces as if to go down the lower path*) I can't stay and hear this ——
Anna I'm sorry, *sorry*.

Maureen stops

I shouldn't have said that. Don't go. Please listen. Please.

Maureen turns to face her

Try to understand. From my point of view? For me, crunch time was when you came out of hospital. Mike promised he would tell you ... but no ... he changed his mind ... you had to be protected and I had to cope as best I could.
Maureen *You* talk about coping? After Thomas died Michael knew I wanted another but the doctor said I couldn't. I pleaded with him to adopt ... but he wouldn't. When I read your email I realized why he was so against it ... it was *you*. A child would be another hold that *I* had on him. Of course he made excuses ... said we were too old ... said he couldn't love another man's child. But the point is, I could have. So you see you both betrayed me in other ways than just infidelity.

Pause

Were you married? Before you met Michael?
Anna (*after hesitating, pacing over to the bench*) Yes ... years before ... disaster ... it lasted two years.
Maureen Children?
Anna No.
Maureen I thought not.
Anna (*crossing to the corner of the bench and stubbing out the cigarette*) Kids? ... That's not my scene.
Maureen We waited fourteen long years to have Thomas.
Anna I'm sorry.

Maureen (*crossing to the bench and releasing all her pent-up emotion*) How can you possibly know? To have created a life ... a life that's growing in you for all that time ... and then to bring it into the world ... to hold it ... To hold it just for a minute. (*She sits, unable to control the tears*) The next time I saw him he was in a coffin ... a little white coffin. It was as if my life was over ... it pushed me over the edge. (*Beat*) When I got home, I thought I was beginning to get better, then while I was on the course I saw the email. I didn't know what to do ... except I had to hold on ... to hold on ...

Anna Couldn't you tell a friend?

Maureen No ...

Anna It could have helped.

Maureen I had my pride. It would have been humiliating. I couldn't admit to anyone that he had this "other life" with you. (*Beat*) You took him from me

Anna (*rising and crossing to the other side of the bench*) So all the blame is on me ... and you exonerate Mike.

Maureen No, I don't. He was weak, gave into temptation.

Anna (*smiling*) I never thought of myself as temptation!

Maureen turns away

Sorry, Maureen. Listen ... listen to me. Perhaps ... at the end of the day he couldn't face up to either of us ... couldn't make the decision. The demands were too great and he couldn't deal with it. I should have realized ... we should have realized.

Maureen The heart attack?

Anna Yes.

Maureen But he'd never had any problems — angina or anything — was he under the doctor?

Anna No, he would have told me.

Maureen He didn't take any medication — in London?

Anna No, he didn't have any. (*Beat*) How did you find out?

Maureen Mr Stafford phoned. Said Michael had just got in after Monday's drive down when he collapsed ... and when

they got him to hospital it was too late. I couldn't take it in ...
just couldn't take it in. (*Beat*) Who told you?
Anna Mike's secretary rang, she was the only one who knew.

Maureen looks at her

About me. I never went to the office.
Maureen Poor Michael. He must have been frightened ... all
on his own ...
Anna Yes ... on his own.

*There is an uncomfortable pause. Anna looks at Michael's
grave*

The roses are lovely. From your garden?
Maureen Yes.
Anna Mike said that you were a keen gardener.
Maureen Did he?

Anna nods

He used to tease me about it. It was something I could take
pride in, but recently I've let it go. (*Beat then quietly*) I've even
stopped bothering about how I look.
Anna Well then ... it's time to start again.

Maureen looks at her

The garden.
Maureen Perhaps I will.

*Maureen takes out small box of pills from her handbag and takes
one out and a small bottle of water. Anna watches and crosses
behind the bench concerned*

Anna Are you all right?

Maureen Yes. (*She swallows the pill*) A few deep breaths and
I'll be fine. (*She does so*) Talking to you hasn't been easy. It
was as if I had been making a confession ... a difficult confession, like when you haven't been for a very long time ... Oh
you want to get it off your chest, you long ... to be forgiven,
but you put it off because you can't face it ... it's all pent up
... inside ... you want to find the words ... the right words, but
you can't. (*Beat*) Are you a Catholic?

Anna No.

Maureen Then it's difficult for you to understand.

Anna I'm lapsed. But I *do* remember.

Maureen looks at her

Confession. Oh yes ... I can understand.

Maureen (*putting the pills and the water back into her bag*) Of
course the priest makes a difference ... if he's a good listener
... has some compassion. Irish ones are the worst — they
simply quote what they learned by rote at the seminary. And
Father Keegan ...

Anna looks at her

Our parish priest ... he isn't easy ... comes from Kildare. (*Beat*)
I sometimes go over to Ilkley, where the priest doesn't know
me ... and that can help.

Anna (*sitting*) What made you come over here?

Maureen looks at her

Maureen Father died, heavily in debt. Gambling. His
retail business had gone. I had to sell the house to pay for
everything.

Anna Didn't you have a job?

Maureen Oh *yes*. I helped in the shop. I looked after the house.
I did the cleaning, the washing, the cooking ... everything.

Anna Why come over to Threshton?

Maureen I had no qualifications. When Mother died I left the convent school before the exams. It was our parish priest who got me the job. He had "connections" ... knew Lady Talbot ... so I crossed the water as they say and came here ... here to the Hall, as housekeeper-companion.

Anna What was it like?

Maureen She wasn't an easy woman, no children. It was a big house, a cold house ... understaffed — but I made a go of it, had to.

Anna And then you met ... Michael.

Maureen And then I met Michael. (*Beat. Quietly*) He was the love of my life. (*Pause*) Did you say you were a student?

Anna Oh, I gave it up.

Maureen Why?

Anna It, er ... it took up too much time. English Lit. All that reading.

Maureen You'll have to start again, pick up where you left off.

Anna I might just do that.

Maureen (*after a pause*) Well ... I'd better go. It's *my* class tonight.

Anna looks at her

A-Level Literature course.

Anna Good, I'm glad ... that you have the class. (*Beat*) Maureen ... I'm sorry ... and I hope in spite of everything ... that for you this is a ... *a beginning*.

Maureen A beginning ... Yes ... I hope so.

Anna (*after a beat*) What are you studying?

Maureen (*smiling*) T. S. Eliot — he's difficult, but we have a good teacher. Eliot makes me think ... he gives me some kind of ...

Anna Reassurance?

Maureen Yes, reassurance. It started off as therapy ... two evenings a week ... and now I love it. Might move on.

Anna Open University?

Maureen You never know.

Anna Go for it. (*Pause*) I'm catching the next bus.

Maureen Quickest way is the top gate. And I go this way. (*She takes a pace towards the lower path*)

Anna It's unlikely that we will meet again...

Maureen (*stopping and turning*) Yes ... unlikely.

Anna Goodbye.

Anna holds out her hand. Eventually Maureen responds

Maureen Goodbye. Go back to your studies. (*She releases her hand*)

Anna I will. And you too.

Maureen nods and goes to the lower path

(*After a moment, calling*) Good luck ...

Maureen, with her back to Anna, stops for a second and then continues waking down the path and exits

(*Quietly*) Good luck.

Anna audibly sighs with the strain of the encounter with Maureen and moves to Michael's grave

That was one for the books. God ... I wasn't prepared ... there were a few lies, had to be ... you would have been proud of me. (*Beat*) It was a kind of ... shriving ... for both of us I suppose, yes ... for both of us. (*Looking towards where Maureen made her exit*) We're so different. Yet I felt sorry for her ... and in spite of everything I liked her ... no, not liked ... admired her. Such resilience and a kind of tenacity ... that was a surprise. (*Beat*) You were a lucky devil. We both loved you, "not wisely, but too well". (*Smiling*) Remember me doing that essay and reading bits of *Othello*? I wasn't very good, but you didn't laugh. (*Angry with herself*) There ... I'm doing it again. You're not here ... *not here*. You've gone. I just can't get it into my head ...

Bob enters from the upper path with the wheelbarrow which is empty apart from his tools

Bob (*calling out*) Anna! Anna it's time you went ...

Anna (*turning to him*) I got detained ... by Maureen.

Bob (*shocked*) I warned you ... I told you not to go that way.

Anna I didn't. She came back, she'd left her gloves.

Bob And?

Anna She knows.

Bob Knows who you are?

Anna Yes.

Bob You told her?

Anna 'Course not. She guessed. She saw a message from me — on Mike's laptop.

Bob I knew she'd been on a course but she never mentioned it ... not a word. (*Beat*) And I thought I really knew her.

Anna Bob, we all choose what *not* to say, what to hold back. (*Meeting his eye*) You should know that.

Bob (*defensively*) She wasn't well.

Anna Yet she's known for six months.

Bob I just can't take it in. (*Beat*) I had to lie, I didn't want to hurt her.

Anna That was Mike's problem, he tried not to hurt anyone, that's what destroyed him.

Pause

Bob You didn't tell Maureen about the lad?

Anna 'Course not. I wanted to, make no mistake about it, I wanted to score. I wanted to say *our* child wasn't stillborn, he's a three-year-old boy and he's beautiful. He's the spitting image of Mike and I'll always have him ... That's what I wanted to say. But I've enough on my conscience without that. There's no need for her to know ... she's suffered enough. (*She meets his eye*) We all have. (*She sighs*) I wonder what she thought of me?

Bob I don't think she'll ever mention it ... not now.

Anna Give her time.

Bob Time wouldn't help ... and not if she knew about Jamie.

Anna Bob ... you chose *not* to tell her. For her sake.

Bob No. (*With strong conviction*) It was a choice I made for Mick. A hard choice but I made it nevertheless.

Anna He was lucky.

Bob (*defensively*) Why?

Anna To have you on his side. (*Beat*) Anyway ... it's time to go. (*She crosses to the bench to collect her handbag*) Come down and see us. Maureen needn't know — tell her it's a big match. It'll be like last year. You'd be welcome ... I mean it. (*Beat*) Mike would want you to.

Bob Would he?

Anna You know he would ... said you were the dad he'd never had.

Bob Did he? (*Trying to hold back the tears*) I'm sorry.

Anna No need. (*She puts her hands on his shoulder*)

Just for a moment, Bob starts to cry

Bob I think about him every time I use this path, every time. With the others ... well ... you get used to it, you detach yourself — you have to. But not with Mick — I miss him. I miss him, Anna.

Anna Yes, I know. I know you do. Take care.

Bob You too.

Anna Are you all right?

Bob Yes. I'm fine.

Pause

Anna (*walking swiftly away via the upper path and calling back to Bob*) And don't forget.

Anna exits

Bob (*calling back*) I won't. (*To the grave*) I meant it, Mick. I will
go down to see them. (*Beat*) I wonder if Anna knows? No. No.
She can't. (*Pause*) Round 'ere they say it's wrong for a man to
love a feller, church certainly doesn't approve, yet there was
nothing I could do. I didn't choose it to happen, Mick, it just
did. When you first turned up ... Monday training night — I
can see you as if it were yesterday ... I don't know how to put
it into words ... I couldn't — get you — out of my head, and
that's where you've stayed. When other people were around I
had to force myself not to look at you ... try not to notice you.
(*Beat*) It wasn't easy, you know, always had to be on my guard
... so that no one knew ... except you ... dear God, I wanted you
to know ... but if I'd told you then I'd never see you again. I
had to be so careful ... rugby team, can you imagine, Mick?
Bloody hell! Then you moved to London. It was the end of my
life. Visit to Twickenham was a bonus ... but it was seeing you
up here *every* Saturday in the pub, just for the hour — that's
what mattered. Little enough, but just enough to shape the
week ... to give it some kind of meaning.

*Bob sees a small section of the drawing that Anna placed under
the chippings. He kneels and picks it up and opens it*

Anna ... (*He shakes his head*) I can't leave this here, you know
I can't. Maureen'll change flowers — can't risk it. (*Rising*) I'll
look after it for you. (*Looking carefully at the drawing*) Your
little bit of immortality ... it's safe with me.

*Bob folds the drawing and puts it in the inside pocket of his
jacket. Bob makes an almost casual sign of the cross and then
lets his arms fall to his side*

We hear a tolling bell as slowly the Lights fade to black-out

FURNITURE AND PROPERTY LIST

On stage: Low headstone with stone surround enclosing
                    grey chippings
            Fixed metal vase containing dead flowers
            Three dried-up wreaths
            Windswept leaves and twigs
            Section of an old Yorkshire stone wall (optional)
            Small branches
            Open meshed litter bin containing rotting flowers and
                    two wreaths
            New roll of plastic wire netting
            Wooden bench. *On it*: enamel jug of water, two
                    bunches of white roses, handbag, shopping
                    basket containining dustpan and brush,
                    plastic bag, newspaper and bottle of water
            Gloves (behind bench)
            Wheelbarrow containing tools and wooden stakes

Personal: **Maureen**: rosary beads
            Anna: handbag containing cigarettes and lighter
                    and child's drawing

Off stage: Handbag containing small box of pills and a small
                    bottle of water (**Maureen**)

LIGHTING PLOT

Practical fittings required: nil

To open: Reduced, intensified lighting on **Bob** and **Maureen** C

Cue 1	**Bob** and **Maureen**: "Amen." (3rd time) *Fade in general exterior lighting*	(Page 2)
Cue 2	**Maureen** pours water in the vase *Reduce and intensify lighting on* **Maureen** C	(Page 9)
Cue 3	**Maureen** exits *Fade in general lighting*	(Page 10)
Cue 4	**Anna** goes to the grave *Reduce and intensify lighting on* **Anna** C	(Page 10)
Cue 5	**Bob** enters *Fade in general lighting*	(Page 10)
Cue 6	**Anna** moves to the grave *Reduce and intensify lighting on* **Anna** C	(Page 13)
Cue 7	**Maureen** enters *Fade in general lighting with warm sunlight on the bench area*	(Page 14)
Cue 8	**Anna** moves to the grave *Reduce and intensify lighting on* **Anna** C	(Page 24)
Cue 9	**Bob** enters *Fade in general lighting*	(Page 25)

| *Cue* 10 | **Bob**: "I won't." | (Page 27) |
| | *Reduce and intensify lighting on* **Bob** c | |

| *Cue* 11 | **Bob** lets his arms fall to his side | (Page 27) |
| | *Fade Lights to black-out* | |

EFFECTS PLOT

Cue 1   To open   (Page 1)
           Distant thunder followed by a tolling bell which fades

Cue 2   **Maureen** exits   (Page 10)
           Sound of rooks, then church clock strikes four

Cue 3   **Bob** lets his arms fall to his side   (Page 27)
           Tolling bell

Printed by The Kingfisher Press, London NW10 7AS